The Illustrated Story of President

JOSEPH SMITH

Great Leaders of The Church
of Jesus Christ of Latter-day Saints

The Illustrated Story of President Joseph Smith
Great Leaders of The Church of Jesus Christ
of Latter-day Saints

Copyright © 1982 by
Eagle Systems International
P.O. Box 5600
Provo, Utah 84603 – 5600

ISBN: 0-938762-01-X
Library of Congress Catalog Card No.: 82-70266

Fourth Printing April 1987

Fifth Printing October 1989

First Edition

A Member of
The American Bookseller's Association
New York, New York

Printed in Singapore

The Illustrated Story of President

JOSEPH SMITH

Great Leaders of The Church
of Jesus Christ of Latter-day Saints

AUTHOR
Della Mae Rasmussen

ILLUSTRATOR
B. Keith Christensen

DIRECTOR AND CORRELATOR
Lael J. Woodbury

ADVISORS AND EDITORS
Paul & Millie Cheesman
Mark Ray Davis
L. Norman Egan
Annette Hullinger
Beatrice W. Friel

PUBLISHER
Steven R. Shallenberger

A
Biography Of
JOSEPH SMITH

"Joseph Smith, the Prophet and Seer of the Lord, has done more, save Jesus only, for the salvation of men in this world, than any other man that ever lived in it. . . ." (D&C 135:3)

This remarkable man was born December 23, 1805, in Sharon, Windsor County, Vermont, to Joseph and Lucy Mack Smith. The family worked hard to earn a living at farming and moved to several different locations in order to do so. In 1819 the family was living in Manchester, New York. Because there was much religious agitation there, Joseph did not know which church to join. He read in the Bible, James 1:5, that those who lack wisdom should ask it of God. When he went to a grove of trees near his home and knelt in prayer, God the Father and his Son Jesus Christ appeared in a pillar of light and told Joseph that the true Church was not found on the earth, and that Joseph would be instrumental in restoring the gospel of Jesus Christ. Joseph was fourteen years old at this time. Three years later an angel named Moroni visited Joseph and told him of ancient gold plates hidden in a nearby hill. Once a year for the next four years Joseph was visited by the angel Moroni. Joseph grew to manhood during these years. At the age of twenty-one he was six feet tall, had a strong, athletic build, light brown hair, and an impressive appearance.

Joseph Smith married Emma Hale on January 18, 1827. A short time later he received the golden plates of the Book of Mormon from Moroni, and Joseph began translating the characters on the plates through the gift and power of God. John the Baptist conferred the Aaronic Priesthood on Joseph and Oliver Cowdery on May 15, 1829. Shortly thereafter the apostles Peter, James, and John appeared to Joseph and Oliver, conferred the Melchizedek Priesthood upon them, and ordained them to the holy apostleship. Joseph finished the translation of the Book of Mormon in June, 1829.

Joseph, with others, organized The Church of Jesus Christ of Latter-day Saints on April 6, 1830. He presided as President of the Church from January 25, 1832, to June 27, 1844.

Although the Church grew rapidly, Joseph suffered much persecution for proclaiming that he had seen a vision. He was arrested many times, tarred and feathered, and mocked by evil people. Still he would not deny what he knew to be true. He and the Saints were driven from their homes and moved from state to state. Finally Joseph gathered his people and established the city of Nauvoo in Illinois. There he was elected mayor in 1842 and declared himself a candidate for President of the United States in 1844.

In June, 1844, Governor Ford of Illinois sent word for Joseph to come to Carthage, Illinois. The governor guaranteed his safety. Joseph knew that his enemies planned treachery, however, and as he left for Carthage with his brother Hyrum and other Brethren, he said, "I am going like a lamb to the slaughter." In Carthage, Joseph and Hyrum were arrested and taken to jail. At about 5:00 p.m. on June 27, 1844, a mob rushed the jail, killing Joseph by gunfire. He was thirty-eight years old.

It is written of Joseph Smith: "He lived great and he died great in the eyes of God and his people. He sealed his mission and his works with his own blood."

Many years ago in a small frame house in Windsor County, Vermont, a great event took place. It was just two days before Christmas in 1805, when a new son was born to Joseph Smith, Sr., and Lucy Mack Smith.

Lucy Smith held her new son close to her and thought, "This is the best Christmas gift a family could ever have." She did not know it, but the baby was a Christmas gift to the whole world, for God had chosen him to be a prophet. This baby boy, Joseph Smith, Jr., was to restore the gospel of Jesus Christ to the earth.

Sometimes people wonder, "What kind of man is chosen by God to be a prophet?" One thing is sure. He must be strong in character, for the life of a prophet is seldom easy. There are always bad people who try to stop the work of the Lord.

Joseph Smith, Jr., was strong in many ways. Two strengths stand out: his unwavering faith and his exceptional courage.

He showed his courage at a very young age. When he was about seven years old, he became very ill with typhus fever. He recovered from the illness, but his leg was left badly infected. The doctor told his parents, "I am afraid Joseph's leg will have to be amputated." His mother begged, "Please, doctor, please try again to save his leg." The doctor finally agreed, saying, "The outcome is doubtful, but I will make the attempt. I will operate, drain the infection, and take out the piece of infected bone."

The doctor turned to the boy. "Joseph," he said, "the operation will be very painful. If you will drink a glass of liquor, it will dull the pain." Joseph answered, "No, I do not want to drink it." The doctor said, "Then we must tie you to the bed so that you will not move about when the pain is very bad." But Joseph answered, "If my father will sit on

8

the bed and hold me in his arms, I will do whatever is necessary to have the bone taken out." So the operation was performed. Remember Joseph was a very young boy! Few grown men would have had such courage. Fortunately, the wound began to heal. His mother took good care of him, but it was nearly a year before Joseph was fully well. He limped for years afterwards.

The Smith family was poor, but they were hardworking, intelligent, and honest. They helped each other, and as soon as Joseph was big enough, he joined his brothers and father to work on the farm. He drove a yoke of oxen to plow the land. Joseph did not have much time for school, but in the evenings, with his mother's help, he learned to read and write and do arithmetic.

When Joseph was ten years old, his father moved the family to Palmyra, New York. Life was still hard for them, but finally his father was able to buy 100 acres of forestland in nearby Manchester, New York. They cleared some land and planted corn, wheat, and sugar maple trees. The father and sons built a log cabin home. It appeared that at last the family had a permanent home.

Joseph grew tall and strong. He was also a pleasant, thoughtful boy. When he was fourteen years old, he noticed that the people around them were very much interested in matters of religion. Meetings were held almost every night in the churches. Each church was trying to get people to join its faith. Joseph's mother, his brothers Hyrum and Samuel, and his sister Sophronia joined one church. Joseph himself became acquainted with a minister of another church but did not join.

Amidst the great excitement the boy Joseph said to himself, "There is so much confusion and strife among the different churches. What is to be done? Who of all these parties is right? Or are they all wrong? If any one of them be right, how shall I know it?" The boy was puzzled. One day he was reading in the family Bible. He came upon the scripture in James 1:5, "If any of you lack wisdom, let him ask of God, that giveth to all *men* liberally, and upbraideth not; and it shall be given him." Joseph said, "Never did any passage of scripture come with more power to the heart of man than this did at this time to mine. It seemed to enter with great force into every feeling of my heart."

Joseph thought, "If any person ever needed wisdom from God, I do. I do not know how to act, and unless I get more wisdom than I have, I will never know."

Then he made a decision that was to change the lives of millions of people for generations to come: "I must either remain in darkness and confusion, or I must do as James directs. I will ask God to give me wisdom!" Joseph had complete faith that God would keep his promise.

Joseph knew of a quiet, beautiful spot in the woods near his home. He thought, "I will go there and make an attempt to get an answer to my question." The morning was clear and lovely, early in the spring of 1820. As he walked toward the woods, he thought, "I have never prayed aloud to God before." Still, he had the faith and courage to kneel alone in the grove of trees. He prayed to God, "What shall I do? Which church is true and which shall I join?" At that moment Joseph was seized by an overwhelming power. Thick darkness gathered around him, and he could not speak. It seemed to Joseph as if he would die at that very instant.

Just when he thought he would not live, he exerted all his strength and called upon God to deliver him from the power of this enemy! At that moment a brilliant pillar of light appeared at a distance in the heavens above his head. The dark power was gone and he was surrounded by the light. He described the pillar of light: "As it drew near, it increased in brightness . . . it was brighter than the noonday sun." Then Joseph was filled with awe. "When the light rested upon me, I saw two Personages, whose brightness and glory defy all description, standing above me in the air. One of them spake, *This is My Beloved Son. Hear Him!*"

When Joseph could speak again, he asked, "Which of the churches is right?" The answer came that he should "join none of them, for they were all wrong. . . . they draw near to me with their lips, but their hearts are far from me. . . ." So Joseph had the answer to his question! The Personage told Joseph many other things too. He said that the true Church of Jesus Christ would again be established upon the earth. If Joseph remained true and faithful, he would be chosen as its leader and prophet.

When the vision was over, Joseph found himself lying on his back looking up into heaven. As he pondered over what had happened, Joseph became very excited. He had learned some things that no one else seemed to know! He knew that:

God does exist.
Jesus Christ is his Son.
Man is created in the image of God.
God and Jesus Christ each have a body of flesh and bones.
God hears and answers prayers.

He thought, "Others will be happy to know what I have seen. It will help clear up the confusion!" He told his mother. She believed him and said, "I have faith in you and your honesty, Joseph. Your vision was indeed from God."

Joseph also told the minister what he knew. But the boy was surprised when the minister said, "There is no truth in what you have told me. . . . There are no such things as visions and revelations in these days. There will never be any more of them." Joseph found he had made a mistake to tell about his wonderful experience. The men from the different religions began to hate and persecute him. Joseph said to his mother, "It is strange that a fourteen-year-old boy should be so hated by the preachers. I feel sad, for I did not want to stir up their dislike for me."

He was laughed at and mocked. Some said, "Joe Smith is a liar." Others scoffed, "The boy is crazy." Here was another time when Joseph showed his courage. He said, "I have seen a vision. I know it. God knows that I know it. I actually did see a light and in it two Personages. They spoke to me. People hate me for saying I have seen a vision. But I know it is true. I cannot deny it."

THINK ABOUT IT:

1. Tell about a time when Joseph showed great faith in the Lord.
2. How did Joseph show his courage?
3. How can you show courage, even when someone might make fun of you?

Except for this bitter opposition, this time in Joseph's life went on as it had before the vision. There were no other unusual experiences for the next three years. On the twenty-first of September, 1823, when he was seventeen years old, he prepared to go to bed. Joseph remembered what the Lord had told him in the first vision. The Lord had said that he would be an instrument to restore Christ's Church to the earth. He wondered why he had received no further instructions. In faith he decided to pray about the matter. As he did so, suddenly a light appeared in the room, growing brighter and brighter until it filled the room like the noonday sun. A heavenly messenger stood before Joseph. The angel wore a loose robe of pure white. His feet did not touch the floor. Joseph described the angel: "His countenance was like lightning. His whole person was glorious beyond description."

The messenger spoke to him, "Joseph, I am Moroni. God has sent me because he has a great work for you to do. Your name shall be had for good and evil among all nations, kindreds, tongues, and people."

The angel Moroni went on to say: "There is a book hidden in a nearby hill. It is written upon gold plates and tells the history of former inhabitants of this continent. The record also contains the fulness of the Savior's everlasting gospel as he taught it to these people." Joseph was listening carefully. The angel continued: "With the record are two stones set in silver bows, fastened to a breastplate. This instrument is called the Urim and Thummim. The stones were known as 'seers' in ancient times. God prepared them for the purpose of translating the book."

Then the angel said, "Joseph, you will be given the plates at a future time, and you will translate them. In the meantime, be patient. Keep yourself worthy to receive them." While the angel was speaking, Joseph saw in a vision the place where the plates were hidden.

The angel left. Joseph lay thinking about what had happened. Suddenly the light again entered the room. The angel appeared the second time and repeated all that he had said before and a little more. Once again the angel left and then appeared the third time, repeating the same message, but again adding some further information."

When the angel Moroni ascended to heaven after his third visit, Joseph heard a rooster crow. The angel's visits had lasted the whole night.

Joseph arose and went with his father to the field. He felt so weak and tired that he could not work. His father said, "Joseph, you do not appear to be well. Go back to the house and rest." Joseph started for the house, but as he tried to climb over a fence, he was so weak that he fell to the ground. He lay unconscious for a time. When he awoke, he looked up and saw the angel Moroni once again.

The angel repeated the instructions of the night before and commanded Joseph to tell his father about the vision and commandments he had received.

Joseph returned to the field where his father was working and told him of the angel's visit. Mr. Smith listened in amazement. He knew that young Joseph would not make up such a story. He knew Joseph was telling the truth. He said, "What you have seen and heard is of God. You must do all that the angel has told you to do."

Joseph left at once for the hill. The date was September 22, 1823. He went straight to the place where the plates were buried, for he had seen the spot in his vision. He told his family later, "I saw a large, flat stone partly covered with earth. I removed the earth. Then I fixed a lever under the edge of the stone and raised it up. I looked into a stone box and there I saw the golden plates, the Urim and Thummim, and the breastplate, as the messenger had told me."

Joseph reached for the plates, but the angel Moroni appeared and said, "The time has not yet come, Joseph. Return to this hill on the same day each year for four years. Then, if you prove faithful, the Lord will permit you to take the plates."

Joseph put the stone lid back on the box. He made a promise. "I will begin to prepare myself. I will try to be obedient to God's commandments. I will need to learn all I can. I will prove myself worthy for the precious plates to be put into my care."

During the next four years Joseph grew to be a powerful, well-built man. He had a fair complexion; light, wavy hair; and a kind, happy face. He was six feet tall and weighed about 200 pounds.

A friend said of him, "He is quick as a squirrel and strong as a mountain lion, but he is gentle as a lamb." Another man remarked, "I have seen him run, jump, wrestle, pitch horseshoes, and pull sticks many times. He is always the winner." Joseph was sociable, cheerful, kind, and hospitable. Joseph had become a man with many fine virtues.

Each year on September 22, Joseph returned to the hill to see the plates and receive instructions from the angel Moroni.

Joseph hired out to earn money to help support his family. He boarded in the home of Isaac Hale, a well-to-do farmer. Mr. Hale had a lovely daughter named Emma. Joseph and Emma fell in love and were married on January 18, 1827. Joseph now had a wonderful companion to love and support him. After their marriage Joseph and Emma moved back to the Smith family farm.

A few months later, on September 22, 1827, it was time to return to the hill. Joseph said to Emma, "I feel fearful, but I also feel great joy, for at last I am to receive the plates." The angel Moroni met Joseph at the hill. The sacred record was placed in Joseph's hands. He turned the leaves of the ancient book. The plates were about eight inches long and six inches wide. They were bound together with three rings. The book was about six inches thick. Part of the record was sealed, so Joseph could not look into it. Engraved on the plates were ancient characters of letters. Joseph also received the Urim and Thummim, through which he was to translate the precious record.

The angel continued to counsel Joseph, saying, "Take the greatest care of the plates. Wicked men will plan and scheme to get them from you. Do not let them pass out of your hands for any reason."

Soon Joseph knew the truth of the angel's words. Evil men tried in every way to steal the plates from him. They ransacked his home and belongings. His life was threatened. Finally Emma said, "Let us go to my father's home, where we can be safe." They had no money for the trip, but the Lord sent help. A man named Martin Harris came to Joseph and said, "I would like to help the work of the Lord by giving you fifty dollars." Joseph thanked him and started out in a wagon for the Hale home in Pennsylvania. On the way wicked men stopped them. They searched the wagon for the plates. They did not find them, for Joseph had hidden them in a barrel of beans. Later Joseph hid the plates in strange places so they would not be stolen. Once he hid them in a rotted birch log, then under a fireplace hearthstone, and another time, under a pile of straw in a barn!

At the home of Emma's parents, Joseph began to translate the characters into the English language. Joseph had little schooling and could not have done such a thing without the help of the Lord.

For a time Martin Harris came to serve as scribe for the Prophet as he translated the plates. One day Martin came to Joseph. He said, "Let me take the manuscript home with me. I would like to show it to my wife and family." Joseph told Martin, "I must inquire of the Lord." This he did, and his request was refused. Martin asked a second time. Joseph went again to the Lord, but the answer was still no. Finally, when Martin asked again, the Lord agreed, "on condition Martin show it only to his brother, his wife, his father and mother, and his wife's sister."

He was warned. "Martin, you must take great care of the manuscript. Do not show it to any others. Do not let it go out of your hands." In spite of this warning Martin lost the precious pages and they were never recovered. After this Joseph was not allowed to work on the translation for some time. He was instructed not to retranslate the pages because evil people would change them and try to call Joseph a fraud. Joseph was told to translate another section of the plates that covered the same period of time. The Lord had made provision for Joseph's mistake hundreds of years before by instructing the ancient writers of the book to make two records of the same time period.

A short time after this a man named Oliver Cowdery came to visit the Prophet Joseph. He was an intelligent, young schoolteacher. He said, "I have heard about the golden plates and have come to find out for myself if the story is true." Oliver was welcomed by Joseph, for he knew by revelation that Oliver was to be his scribe.

On May 15, 1829, Joseph translated a section about baptism. He and Oliver prayed for guidance about the right and authority to perform baptisms. A heavenly messenger appeared and said, "I am John the Baptist. I am thy fellow servant." He laid his hands upon Joseph and Oliver and conferred the Priesthood of Aaron upon them, giving them the right to baptize by immersion for the remission of sins. He told Joseph to baptize Oliver and instructed Oliver to baptize Joseph. Soon others came forward to be baptized, including Samuel and Hyrum, the Prophet's brothers.

A short time after Joseph and Oliver received the Aaronic Priesthood, they were visited by the apostles Peter, James, and John. These ancient apostles conferred the Melchizedek Priesthood, or higher priesthood, upon Joseph and Oliver. It was necessary that this priesthood be restored to give men the authority to act for God on this earth.

Many exciting events were taking place one after the other. It was made known to Joseph that three special witnesses were to be shown the gold plates by the power of God. Oliver Cowdery, David Whitmer, and Martin Harris were the three chosen to be the special witnesses. An angel showed the plates to these three men and turned the gold leaves so they could see the engraved characters. A voice said to them, "These plates have been revealed and translated by the power of God. The translation which you have seen is correct, and I command you to bear record of what you now see and hear."

Joseph went to his father's home. He exclaimed, "Father, Mother, you do not know how happy I am. The Lord has now caused the plates to be shown to three more besides myself. They have seen an angel, who has testified to them. They will have to bear witness to the truth of what I have said, for now they know for themselves that I do not go about to deceive the people. I feel as if I were relieved of a burden which was almost too heavy for me to bear. It rejoices my soul that I am no longer entirely alone in the world!"

Later Joseph was commanded to show the plates to eight more witnesses.

The Book of Mormon was now translated and needed to be published. Joseph did not know how to raise the needed money. Martin Harris, his loyal friend, came forward and offered to mortgage his farm to pay for the printing. The first edition of 5,000 copies was printed for the sum of 3,000 dollars.

A few weeks later Joseph received a revelation that he was to organize The Church of Jesus Christ. Six men gathered on Tuesday, April 6, 1830. They were Oliver Cowdery, Joseph Smith, Jr., Hyrum Smith, Peter

Whitmer, Jr., Samuel H. Smith, and David Whitmer. The Lord told Joseph
how the Church should be organized. Joseph was sustained as Prophet,
Seer, and Revelator.

More and more people, including Joseph's family and friends, were
converted to the gospel of Jesus Christ and were baptized into the Church.
By the first of June, 1831, the membership of the Church was nearly 2,000.

33

This success caused evil men to increase their attacks against the Prophet and the new Church. On a dark night in March, 1832, a mob dragged Joseph from his bed. He was taken to a field, beaten, and covered with tar and feathers. Joseph thought he would

certainly lose his life that night. Joseph told of his experience, "My friends spent the rest of the night in scraping and washing my body, so that by morning I was ready to be clothed again. It was the Sabbath and people gathered for meeting at the usual hour. I recognized some of the mobsters in the audience. With my flesh all scarified and defaced, I preached to the congregation, as usual, and in the afternoon of the same day baptized three individuals." What an example of Joseph's faith and courage!

The stronger the Prophet became and the larger the Church grew, the more he was bitterly hated and persecuted by his enemies. Even some of the men he loved and trusted turned against him. They left the Church and became his enemies. Joseph must have felt lonely and sad many times, but he continued on with faith and courage. He was determined to do the work of the Lord, no matter what he had to endure.

Through it all, Joseph continued ever-loving and generous. One time his wife exclaimed, "Mr. Smith can never eat without his friends!" Joseph said, "If any man is hungry, let him come to me and I will feed him at my table. If any are hungry or naked . . . come and tell me and I will divide with them to the last morsel. . . ."

Joseph had unwavering faith in prayer. At one time Joseph and Emma sat down to eat a sparse meal of corn bread. He prayed, "Lord, we thank thee for this johnnycake and ask thee to send something better. Amen." Just as they began to eat, a man knocked on the door and said, "I have brought you some flour and a ham." "Thank you," said Joseph, "and I bless you for the gift." The Prophet turned to his wife and exclaimed, "I knew the Lord would answer my prayer."

Mobs were determined to drive the Mormons out of Missouri. The Prophet had to find another home for his people. They chose a section of land near Commerce, Illinois. They named the new town Nauvoo, which meant "beautiful city." Hundreds of families driven from Missouri came to the new place of safety. The land was swampy and had to be drained. It was home to millions of mosquitoes, and many of the Saints became ill with fever. Even though Joseph himself was sick, he was very concerned about his people. On July 22, 1839, he got up from his sickbed and went among the Saints. Wherever he visited, he healed the sick and they arose from their beds. He came to the home of Elijah Fordham, who was so ill his family thought he would soon die. The Prophet took Brother Fordham's hand. He looked at the sick man for a long time. Brother Fordham seemed to regain consciousness. Joseph asked, "Do you know me?" "Yes," came the faint answer. "Brother Fordham, do you have the faith to be healed?"

"I fear it is too late."

"Do you believe in Jesus Christ?"

"I do."

Joseph stood tall. He said in a loud voice, "Brother Fordham, I command you in the name of Jesus Christ to arise from this bed and be made whole." Brother Fordham got up from his bed. He kicked the bandages off his feet, put on his clothes, and ate a bowl of bread and milk. Then he followed the Prophet into the street. This and other mighty miracles were performed by the Prophet Joseph Smith.

THINK ABOUT IT:

1. What did Joseph have to do before he could receive the plates?

2. What mistake did Joseph make that resulted in 116 pages of the manuscript being lost?
3. What were some of the things that Joseph did that show he was a true prophet of God?

Nauvoo grew rapidly and became the largest city in Illinois. The Prophet called the Brethren as missionaries to go out into the world to spread the gospel. For a time the Saints were free from persecution and lived in peace. Joseph instructed many brethren in the School of the Prophets. He organized the Nauvoo Legion, a military body, to protect the people. Music and drama were encouraged. Joseph was happy and told the Saints, "Two years ago mobs were threatening, plundering, driving, and murdering us. They burned our homes. They sent our women and children homeless into the streets. Now we enjoy peace and can accomplish the Lord's work."

But all too soon the persecution began again. Thirty-eight times in fourteen years Joseph was seized and charged with murder, treason, and other crimes. No accusation was ever proven to be true. At one time Joseph and some of his brethren were arrested and held prisoners in a vacant house in Richmond, Missouri. The guards were laughing and talking in foul and evil language. They were boasting about hurting and killing Mormon men, women, and children.

At last the Prophet could stand it no longer. Although he was chained, he stood up to his full height and cried out, "Silence, ye fiends of the infernal pit! In the name of Jesus Christ, I rebuke you and command you to be still. I will not live another minute and hear such language. Cease such talk or you or I die this instant." The guards were stunned at the prisoner's courage. They dropped their guns and asked his pardon. They said not another word.

Joseph's persecutions continued to increase. He had hardly a moment of peace. Brigham Young described this time in Joseph's life: "If you were to put one rabbit on Temple Square with 1,000 hounds, that was what it was like for Joseph to live."

In June, 1844, some of his enemies gathered near Carthage, Illinois. Newspaper headlines called for all of the Mormons to be driven out or killed. Joseph said to his brother, "Hyrum, take your family away." Hyrum replied, "Joseph, I will not leave you."

The governor of Illinois sent word to Joseph to come to Carthage. He promised Joseph the full protection of the state of Illinois. Joseph agreed to come. On the way he remarked to his brethren, "I am going like a lamb to the slaughter, but I am calm as a summer's morning. I have a conscience void of offense toward God and toward all men."

When they arrived in Carthage, they were arrested for treason. Joseph and Hyrum, along with Apostles John Taylor and Willard Richards, were taken to the county jail. On June 27, 1844, about five o'clock in the afternoon, a mob of armed men, with blackened and painted faces, gathered at the jail. The guards ran away, and the wicked men climbed the stairs to the jail room. The Brethren tried to hold the door shut against them, but the murderers pushed the door partly open and fired their guns into the room. Hyrum was struck by a bullet and fell, crying out, "I am a dead man." When Hyrum fell, Joseph cried, "Oh, my dear brother, Hyrum!" Joseph turned from the door and sprang toward the window. Instantly two bullets pierced him from the door. Another bullet struck him from outside, and he fell from the window to the ground, exclaiming, "Oh Lord, my God." A great prophet lay dead.

When people think of Joseph Smith, they admire his accomplishments. He was a city-planner, an army leader, mayor of a city, a candidate for U.S. President, and a prophet of the Lord. He received revelations, translated sacred records, performed miracles, spoke prophecies, and restored Christ's true Church to the earth.

He was known everywhere as a man of power. A stranger could recognize him among a great crowd of people as a prophet of God. His faith and courage stand as a beacon for his people. Finally, he sealed his testimony with his death.

TESTIMONY

And now, after the many testimonies which have been given of him [Jesus Christ], this is the testimony, last of all, which we give of him: That he lives!

For we saw him, even on the right hand of God; and we heard the voice bearing record that he is the Only Begotten of the Father——

That by him, and through him, and of him, the worlds are and were created, and the inhabitants thereof are begotten sons and daughters unto God. (D&C 76:22-24)